Pyne's Royal Residences

JOHN CORNFORTH

Folio Miniatures

MICHAEL JOSEPH
London

FOLIO MINIATURES
General Editor: John Letts

First published in Great Britain by
Michael Joseph Ltd
52 Bedford Square
London WC1B 3EF
1976

© *1976 John Cornforth*

ISBN 0 7181 1476 0

The Endpaper: King George III and Queen Charlotte:
Portrait Medallions by Josiah Wedgwood (*Josiah
Wedgwood Museum*)

PRINTED AND BOUND IN BELGIUM
by Henri Proost & Cie p.v.b.a., Turnhout

Introduction

'Her poor to *palaces* Britannia brings,
St James's *hospital* may serve for Kings.'

So quoted J. P. Malcolm at the start of his description of St James's Palace in 1807 (in *London Redivivum* Vol IV). And he went on to say that although poets were generally believed to deal in fiction, in this case they were speaking the truth. 'The vast Palace of Westminster is now a sad memento of past splendour. Whitehall is reduced to a chapel; Somerset-house to dust. Kensington lies in utter neglect. Buckingham-house was merely the residence of a duke; and the site of the palace of St James has been that of a Hospital for lepers, or persons afflicted with the horrible disorder termed the leprosy. Greenwich and Chelsea Hospitals confirm the assertion in the first line: that superannuated sailors and soldiers deserve those palaces no Briton will deny; but surely every Briton must wish to see his Sovereign more splendidly lodged.'

To read this must have been sweet music to the Prince Regent, but in fact there had been no lack of schemes for a Royal Palace during the previous two hundred years, and none were more ambitious than the series of abortive projects for a new Whitehall Palace produced by Inigo Jones for Charles I, one of which was scarcely dry when the King was executed in 1649. English architecture might have taken a rather different course if Inigo Jones's Whitehall had been built, or if William Talman or William Kent or William

3

Chambers had had their chance. However, the reasons why they did not are a complex mixture of constitutional history, the characters of the monarchs themselves and, of course, the shortness of their purses. Charles I, Charles II and William and Mary all had great architectural ambitions, but none of them actually managed to complete a palace they had begun; and indeed it was left to Edward VII to complete Buckingham Palace in the opening years of this century. Surely this is a curious history. But then considering all those splendid 18th century English folios on architecture, it is also equally surprising that the first properly illustrated survey of the royal palaces and houses was only produced in 1820, and then as a part work.

It is to this project rather than to the palaces and residences themselves that this little book is devoted. That is why it is called *Pyne's Royal Residences* and not just *Royal Residences*, with Pyne's name in small print. 'Part works' were not a publishing invention of the 1960s, but anyone running their eye along a library shelf and coming on the three volumes of W. H. Pyne's *The History of the Royal Residences of Windsor Castle, St James's Palace, Carlton House, Kensington Palace, Hampton Court, Buckingham House, and Frogmore*, dedicated to Queen Charlotte, the Prince Regent and the Duke of York, could be excused if they did not see them as one of the ancestors of *The Human Body* in 104 instalments or *Great Wars* in 208. W. H. Pyne was a talented watercolourist who attempted to turn to publishing in the wake of Rudolph Ackermann, and is now principally remembered for his record of the royal residences in the last years of King George III.

Individual plates from the series of one hundred that he commissioned are frequently reproduced, but the project as a whole deserves consideration from several points of view: as a publishing venture, as a record of the tastes of the King, Queen Charlotte and the Prince Regent, as an insight into contemporary attitudes to the past, and as evidence of current fashions in decoration.

4

Our knowledge about all these subjects has changed in recent years, and this applies particularly to the King and Queen themselves, first through the study of the King's illness and then through their new biographies, *King George III* by John Brooke (1972) and *Queen Charlotte* by Olwen Hedley (1975), and by the exhibition *George III Collector and Patron* held at The Queen's Gallery in 1974–75. Mr Brooke's and Miss Hedley's books make it possible to get much more out of Pyne's project than seemed possible even five years ago.

This may sound like an attempt to make a mountain out of a molehill, or four steps towards a PhD, but having had the plates of Carlton House brought to life for me as a school-boy by Sacheverell Sitwell in *British Architects and Craftsmen* and looked lately at others from different points of view, I was surprised to see Pyne's project as yet another instance of that marriage of art and industry which is such a fascinating aspect of George III's reign. The names of Boulton and Wedgwood are synonymous with this development, but they were by no means alone, and it is now clear that the King had a strong sense of his position as a fount of patronage; moreover he was a very active bibliophile, as can be seen from his noble library, which was given by George IV to the British Museum. If George III had lived to enjoy good health in his later years, he would have surely taken great pleasure in seeing how the development of the tradition of the topographical water-colour coincided with the perfecting of the aquatint process and made a new kind of book possible.

First developed in France by J. B. Le Prince (1734–81), aquatinting was taken up in England by Paul Sandby about 1775 and soon widely adopted. It was a near-ideal technique for reproducing watercolours, or rather for providing a base for reproductions; and from the early 1790s until the late 1820s, when lithography began to be fashionable, a spate of very fine books illustrated with coloured aquatints was produced to satisfy the new interests in travel and antiquities.

Basically a form of etching, aquatinting works on the same

principle of using acid on a prepared plate, but whereas in etching the artist draws through the wax into the plate and the acid then bites through the scored wax following the line of the point, the plate for aquatinting is prepared with resinous powder or sand and the acid works through it, creating a finely granulated surface; and variety of tone is achieved by repetitions of the process. The illustrations were printed from one or two plates and then coloured in watercolour by teams of carefully directed artists. Among the celebrated early books were Farington's *History of the River Thames* published by Boydell in 1794 at 10gns and James Malton's *Picturesque and Descriptive Views of the City of Dublin*, but it was Rudolph Ackermann who really succeeded in the commercial development of aquatint illustrations.

Having run a drawing school apparently quite successfully from about 1795 to 1806, he opened a library for art books at 101 The Strand, acting as a publisher and printseller as well as a dealer in artist's materials and fancy articles. In 1808 he went into 'part works' illustrated with hand-coloured aquatint prints, his first venture being *The Microcosm of London*, employing as his artists Augustus Charles Pugin, an emigré French artist and well known as an architectural draughtsman, (the father of A. W. N. Pugin, the Victorian architect) and Thomas Rowlandson. Having planned the project to consist of twenty-four numbers at 7/6d. each, he increased the total to twenty-six and the price to 10/6d. The three complete volumes came out in 1810 at 13gns. By the time they appeared, he had began to publish his magazine *The Repository of the Arts* at 4s. a month and then he went on to do a series of finely illustrated books on Westminster Abbey (1812), Moscow (1813), Oxford (1813), and Cambridge (1814).

Pyne never operated on such a scale; nor was he so successful. Having started out as a watercolourist and exhibited at the Royal Academy from 1790, his first book was *The Costume of Great Britain* which he wrote and illustrated (but did not publish). The first edition appeared in 1804, a second in 1808,

6

which was described as a 'nine-guinea show box' among other things in *The Monthly Review*, and a third in 1819–20. He had some connection with Ackermann, but with his *Royal Residences* he started on his own, publishing the first part on 4th June, 1816. He wrote the text, commissioned a number of watercolourists and engravers and chose Harrison of the Strand (who had worked on several occasions for Ackermann) as his printer. The dedication to the Queen in Volume I is dated June 1817, and to the Prince Regent in Volume II, June 1818.

But by that time Pyne must have been getting into difficulties because in December 1818 his name as publisher was replaced on some of the plates by that of A. Dry of 36 Upper Charlotte Street, and by February 1819 Pyne was giving Upper Charlotte Street as his address. The *Dictionary of National Biography* records that he was imprisoned for debt, so presumably he had to sell out to Dry, and it is the latter's name that appears as the publisher of the completed volumes. By the time they came out in July 1820 (at £25 4s. for the quarto edition or £37 16s. for that on large paper) both the Queen and the King were dead, and so the books got caught up in a flood of *memorabilia* about the old king and his court.

Of the hundred plates, fifty-nine are from drawings by C. Wild, twenty-five by Stephanoff, nine by Cattermole, six by Westall and one by Samuel, but what is remarkable is their uniformity of style. Perhaps they do not have quite the sureness of Pugin's architectural draughtsmanship or the brilliance and dash of Rowlandson's figures, so successfully combined together in *The Microcosm of London*; Pyne's artists had to cope with what struck contemporaries as dim, ponderous chambers in several of the palaces; but for all that they are a very remarkable achievement. When one encounters an uncoloured copy like that in the library of the Society of Antiquaries of London, it is interesting to see how Pyne gave added life to the exterior views by using a blue plate for sky and a brown plate for the rest of the view and for interiors.

House and Carlton House in London. And soon after his marriage George III was able to buy Buckingham House for Queen Charlotte for £28,000 out of the Privy Purse. Here they made their home, altering it initially and then enlarging it to house their increasing family and the even faster-growing royal library. In 1776 the King gave his consort Queen Anne's old Garden House at Windsor, and there in the late 1770s below the south front of the castle, Chambers raised a large castellated house called the Queen's Lodge. Later George decided to make more use of the castle itself, some alterations being done there in the late 1770s and early 1780s, and then a great deal more after 1800.

Meanwhile in the early 1780s, on his coming of age, the Prince of Wales established himself at Carlton House where the Duke of York's column now stands at the bottom of Lower Regent Street. In 1793 the Queen bought Frogmore as a retreat convenient for Windsor. Here she employed James Wyatt, a choice that led to his succeeding Chambers as Surveyor General in 1796. It was in his official capacity that Wyatt embarked on the transformation of Windsor Castle, which was sufficiently advanced for the Royal Family to occupy in 1804, and also on the new Kew Palace, which was abandoned as an unfinished shell in 1811. The Prince Regent seemed to be running through a host of architects – Henry Holland, William Porden, Thomas Hopper, John Nash and several Wyatts – and was up to his eyes in building – and debts – at Brighton, Carlton House and Royal Lodge, Windsor.

Unfortunately the state of the royal residences on George III's death was still unsatisfactory, and the new King had a good case when he embarked on a new Buckingham Palace. Neither the Queen's House, as it had been known, nor Carlton House were suited to serve as royal palaces and private residences, and the private apartments at St James's had been burnt in 1809 and not rebuilt. Hampton Court had been given up to grace-and-favour apartments; the only house left at Kew was the 17th century Dutch House; and at Kensington

The Royal children, Windsor Castle in the background. Detail from a portrait of Queen Charlotte by Benjamin West (By Gracious Permission of Her Majesty the Queen)

George IV not only had memories of his dreaded wife, Caroline of Brimswick, who had lived there, but he had installed his brother, the Duke of Kent, who complained in 1814: 'I cannot keep a single piece of meat in my larder, from the rain pouring through the ceiling at twenty different points, and I am literally perishing with cold in my library.' Carlton House and the shell of Kew were both to go during George IV's reign; if he had had his way, St James's would have gone too.

However, money had been spent at St James's on the state rooms in 1794 in preparation for his wedding and again after the fire of 1809, so the Government opposed the idea. The old palace may not have been impressive: indeed, as L. Simond wrote in 1815: 'It is impossible to conceive anything worse of the palace kind.' But, as Pyne said: 'The number, succession and proportions of its apartments are such for every display of regal state and ceremonial connected with a court, that it may be said, we believe, to rival the most admired palaces of foreign princes.'

The display Pyne had in mind was that of levées and drawing-rooms, which had been regular functions until the breakdown of the King's health, and occasional events such as the reception of an ambassador and a court ball. Today the only one of these to survive is the reception of an ambassador: indeed there are now a great many more ambassadors accredited to 'the Court of St James's', as it is still known, and quite frequently processions of closed landaus drawn by pairs of horses are to be seen taking ambassadors and members of their embassy to present their Letters of Credence or Recall to Her Majesty at Buckingham Palace. Investitures and garden parties are modern innovations and replace the earlier idea of attendance at court as being a way of paying one's respects to the monarch.

Levées were purely male occasions held by the King and until his illness, they took place regularly on Wednesdays and Fridays (and until 1788 on Mondays when Parliament was sitting) in the morning at St James's Palace. Having mounted the stairs to the King's Guard Chamber, one entered first the Presence Chamber and then the Privy Chamber; here there was a choice of direction with the Little Drawing Room and State Bedchamber to the left and the Large Drawing Room and Council Chamber to the right. Pyne illustrates the Presence Chamber with its canopy of state under which the King could occasionally receive formal addresses, and one has to visualise turning left in the Privy Chamber to attend a levée, the King entering the State Bedroom from his Closet, where he granted audiences to his ministers.

He 'did' the circle that formed for him in the drawing room and was expected to speak to everyone, attendance being more or less compulsory for those prominent in public life. How long it all took depended on the number of people there, but the King might well be on his feet continuously from 11.00 until 5.00 without refreshment, holding first his levée and then giving audiences. The purpose was partly ceremonial in that it consisted of presentations of individuals to the monarch, but it also related to the business of government as it was the occasion when addresses and petitions were presented and offices were given out.

Drawing-rooms were a weekly event on Thursdays and were attended by both men and women. They took place in the morning and were held in the rooms to the right of the Privy Chamber. In the earlier years of George III's reign when the King and Queen were in London a drawing-room was also generally held after church on Sundays; later the Queen held them at the Queen's House, and after his mother's death the Prince Regent followed his great-grandfather's precedent after the death of his Queen Caroline and held them at Carlton House. However, as Lady Susan O'Brien reminds us, there were great changes between 1760 and 1818: writing of the earlier years, 'Drawing-rooms once a week. Very select company; that is, few without titles or offices or connexions at court; on some occasions crowded drawing-rooms, but in a well regulated and elegant assembly of the best company,' and later, 'Now held but 2 or 4 times a year, and everybody man or woman that assumes the name of gentleman or lady go to it. The crowds are so great and so little decorum attended to that people's clothes are literally torn to pieces.'

This is hardly the impression given by Ackermann's plate in the *Microcosm* dated 1809, but court dresses throughout George III's reign tended to have unwieldy wide hooped skirts and the feathers worn meant that often the roof of a sedan chair had to be open (because of the crush many ladies preferred to go to St James's in a chair rather than in a carriage). The most crowded days were Birthdays, and Richard Rush, the American ambassador, describes the drawing-room held on Queen Charlotte's birthday at the Queen's House in 1817. There the Queen's rooms had always been on the first floor, and early in the century James Wyatt had constructed a new staircase within the painted walls which dated from the time of the builder of the house, John Sheffield, Duke of Buckingham. This 'branched off at the first landing with two arms wide enough to admit a partition. So the company ascending took one channel, those descending the other, but all stood motionless, the hoop dresses of the ladies sparkling with lama plumes, lappets in confusion. In three quarters of an hour we gained the top of the staircase. Four rooms were allotted to the ceremony; in the second was the Queen, then aged seventy-six. She sat on a red velvet chair and cushion a little raised, and near her the Princesses and ladies in waiting. The general company bowed and passed by . . . No lady was without her plume, the whole was a waving field of feathers; some were blue, some tinged with red; here you saw violet and yellow, there shades of green, but most were like tufts of snow; the diamonds encircling them caught the sun and threw dazzling beams around . . .'

On occasions such as these the relative simplicity of the state rooms at St James's did not matter: one could not see the rooms anyway. Today, however, when one goes to Hampton Court and walks through the two series' of state rooms, the King's and the Queen's sides, that it is virtually impossible to imagine early 18th century court life: they still have the melancholy they possessed throughout George III's reign. Instead it is happier to think of George III in the 1790s as the first commuter, as John Brooke describes him, driving at great speed to Windsor on Sunday evening for three nights, then going to London via Kew on Wednesday, staying one night at the Queen's House and then returning to Kew after

Ancient Bell Tower, Windsor Castle: drawn by Cattermole

the drawing-room on Thursday. Both the King and Queen carried out their court duties with great punctiliousness and the King worked conscientiously on his government business, but what they liked was the comparatively simple life that the Queen's House, Kew, the Queen's Lodge at Windsor and Frogmore afforded them.

The Plates

To distil sixteen plates from one hundred does an inevitable injustice to the sweep of Pyne's project, but the selection has been made in order to give some idea of the kind of record that he made for his contemporaries. Virtually the whole of the first volume is devoted to Windsor Castle, with only a short final chapter on Frogmore. The main importance of the Windsor plates is as a record of the state rooms formed for Charles II by Hugh May with their painted decorations by Verrio, whom Pyne describes as 'a wag who perpetuated his private pique without respect to persons . . .', and a great deal of carving by Grinling Gibbons.

Compared with Versailles with its lavish use of coloured marbles, the wainscoted rooms at Windsor fitted out in the 1670s must have always seemed rather sober, but in fact they were the first Baroque interiors designed in England and their conception inspired the parade rooms in such late 17th-century houses as Chatsworth, Burghley and Boughton, and indeed Hampton Court. Something of their character still survives in the King's Dining Room, the Queen's Audience Chamber and the Queen's Presence Chamber, but the balance of the whole scheme was upset by Wyatville when he did his great remodelling in the 1820s; and it is a matter of lasting regret that he destroyed both the Royal Chapel and St George's Hall, for they were the climax of Charles II's palace.

The Hall depicted the Black Prince's triumphal reception by Edward III and Charles II in Garter robes enthroned in glory, and the Chapel walls and ceiling were integrated through Verrio's design, so that the eyes of worshippers travelled from scenes of Christ's miracles seen behind a colonnade to the Resurrection of Christ on the ceiling. Behind the altar was a Last Supper framed by columns inspired by Bernini's *baldacchino* in St Peter's, Rome with gilded capitals and vast swags of flowers. From Pyne's plate (*b*) it is not clear how much of all this was *trompe-l'oeil* and how much carved and gilded wood, but documents show that Gibbons did a great deal of carving in the chapel in 1680–2, working mainly on the decoration behind the stalls and on the King's seat. Of this superb work all that survives are some sprays of palm and laurel re-used in the Waterloo Chamber. Even in Pyne's day the Chapel was already partially dismantled, and now it is only in the chapel at Chatsworth that one gets a sense of the grandeur May achieved at Windsor.

For about a century the state rooms remained more or less intact, but in the 1780s George III made various alterations, particularly in his Audience Chamber (*c*). Here he kept Verrio's ceiling, representing the re-establishment of the Church of England at Charles II's restoration, and also the contemporary cornice, but the latter was gilded and the rest of the room changed. The walls were hung with Garter-blue velvet with borders of flowers, and Benjamin West provided a series of pictures depicting the reign of Edward III. However the dominating feature of the room was the new canopy and chair of state, the former having a richly carved and gilded cornice with valances decorated with garlands of flowers designed by Mary Moser and worked by Mrs Pawsey's school of needlework. The embroidery must have been of very fine quality judging by that on Queen Charlotte's bed now at Hampton Court, which was embroidered by Mrs Pawsey's aunt, Mrs Wright, and set up in 1778. A new chim-

The Ball Room at Windsor (detail) : *drawn by C. Wild*

neypiece together with a steel grate was installed in 1786, and this is shown complete with its curved fender fitting neatly into the opening and leaving most of the hearthstone free.

Two of what must have been a series of three chandeliers appear and they are of an elegant airy design, hung as was usual on counterweights hidden by red tassels so that they could be lowered for the replacement of candles. Wax candles were expensive, and even in the Royal Household, where it was usual to light candles only once and for the ends to be a servant's perquisite, it is likely that the size of candle selected for use was dictated by the expected length of the occasion; in 1830 it was recorded that candles weighing four to the pound lasted 11 hours and those weighing six to the pound lasted six or seven hours.

There is nothing very domestic about the Windsor interiors that Pyne shows us, and indeed at the time he was working on the book the castle must have been a melancholy place, the old King being blind and deaf as well as apparently deranged. Naturally he glosses over all this and depicts instead the happier side of the Queen's life in his plates of Frogmore, which had begun as a middling-large country house of evidently considerable charm and no great pretension.

The exterior view (d) shows the lake laid out by Major William Price, the Queen's Vice-Chamberlain and the brother of Sir Uvedale Price, the author of *An Essay on the Picturesque*, and the colonnade added on to the house by James Wyatt because the Queen wanted one 'which will make a sweet retirement in the summer all Dressed out with Flowers'. It is not entirely clear how often the Queen stayed in the house or whether she merely used to spend days there pursuing her different interests. Here she kept her botanical collections, and also many of her books and even a printing press, and Princess Elizabeth worked away at japanned decorations.

Pyne did not illustrate the room painted by Mary Moser, which is the only interior to survive more or less intact, but the Library as it was shown in the plate published in 1817 and the

Dining Room as shown in a plate published two years later are typical fashionable interiors of their day. The Library (*e*) was one of the rooms added on by Wyatt, but its plasterwork seems very simple for the 1790s so the room may well have been altered after that when the curtains were replaced. The walls appear to have been painted a shade of brown to tone with the satinwood graining of the bookcases, doors and shutters. No white seems to have been used, even for the window frames; the glazing bars and all the mouldings were evidently a dark brown, and the door architraves darker still. The curtains were a combination of two materials, a patterned green stuff and a plain light brown, and there were blinds of a type now usually called Roman shades. (They work on cords but instead of hanging in festoons they draw up into pleats.) Case covers in the green of the curtains are shown on the chairs and the carpet is fitted to the room, probably being a strip carpet sewn together and then given a border. Among the small details of interest are the placing of the davenport in front of the chair beside the fire, the library chair and steps combined which are close to a recorded design of about 1810, and the Chinese jardinière filled with plants on the floor in front of the window.

Pyne describes the Dining Room (*f*) as 'fitted up in a style of elegant simplicity, in conformity with the notions of her Majesty'. Its dominant feature was the three pairs of curtains, with an elaborate continued drapery, again of two materials, a red and a white, linking them together. The curtains themselves were white, but edged with a deep bobbin fringe picking up the red, and the red was continued in the seats of the chairs. These are ranged round the walls, and over the table is a green cloth, but the lack of candles in the chandeliers and earlier silver sconces suggests that the room had not been much used after the Queen's death the previous autumn. Just below the architrave a rod was fixed for the pictures and they were each hung on four cords, so forming a pattern.

The combination of past and present is continued in the second

The Green Pavilion, Frogmore (detail): *drawn by C. Wild*

volume, for it is devoted to Hampton Court, Buckingham House (the Queen's House) and Kensington Palace.

It was almost sixty years since the state rooms at Hampton Court had been used by the Sovereign, and in the years to come George IV was to regard the place as little more than a quarry for statues. One of its few admirers was the Duke of Sussex; William IV called it 'the quality poor house' on account of such distinguished residents as Lady Mornington, the mother of the Duke of Wellington who lived there from 1795. However it was open to visitors, and after free opening was instituted in 1838, no less than 115,971 people came in 1839, the highest total of 236,000 being recorded in 1882. Although George III did not use the palace – indeed, it seems he made a conscious decision not to – he had a strong feeling for historical relics and, just as he kept Queen Anne's bed of cut velvet at Windsor, Queen Mary's crimson damask bed was kept at Hampton Court. Both are now on view at Hampton Court, but documents show that in fact the so-called Queen Mary's bed was made in 1715, just over twenty years after her death, for George, Prince of Wales. Pyne's illustration (a) is of particular interest because he shows it protected by case curtains, which were invariably put up round state beds from the late 17th century onwards to protect them. Although often mentioned in bills and inventories, they are virtually never seen today and yet it was their use that explains why such beds have survived; they were usually of the same colour as the bed but of a cheaper material or they were of the same stuff as the lining of the bed curtains. The chandelier shown is one of the three of rock crystal at Hampton Court; its silver frame was supplied as late as 1736.

Both in this room and in the First Presence Chamber or Throne Room (g) one point that must strike a modern eye is the hanging of pictures over tapestry, a tradition that now survives only in the Long Gallery at Hardwick Hall. In Pyne's view the fireplace is flanked by a large Tintoretto and a large Palma, and the Tintoretto has now migrated two rooms along the suite to the King's Audience Chamber. Canopies still survive in both rooms, the one in the First Presence Chamber being the one depicted by Pyne.

The appearance of these canopies raises questions about the use of these rooms, which was already partly forgotten by Pyne's day, as can be seen from his title to the plate: it was not really the Throne Room, but was the second room of the state apartment, the first being the Great Chamber or King's Guard Chamber at the head of the King's stairs. Once the Great Chamber had become identified with being a guard chamber, the two Presence Chambers also lost some of their importance, and the Audience Chamber became the chief room: it had been planned by Wren as the Drawing Room, and the present Drawing Room was originally the Ante-Room to the Bedchamber. There would have always been canopies in the Presence and Audience Chambers, but as court etiquette changed the monarch tended to receive further and further back in the apartment so that his court could be accommodated in the outer rooms. However, all passing a canopy were expected to bow as a mark of reverence to the monarch.

The Queen's House was not an official palace but even so Queen Charlotte had her chair of state and canopy in the Saloon (h), a room redecorated by Sir William Chambers evidently soon after its purchase by the King. However, here there was not a full apartment as at Hampton Court, and in 1776 Chambers pierced the south wall so that there could be direct access from the head of the main stairs into it. The room itself was a recasting of the Duke of Buckingham's original Saloon, but it is not clear how much of the decoration shown by Pyne dates from the early 1760s and how much from a generation later. Cipriani's ceiling was part of the original scheme for the Queen but, as the Raphael Cartoons hung here from 1763 until 1787 and the chimneypiece was made by Bacon in 1789, it seems likely that the articulation of the walls with French-looking pilaster strips must date from that time; it may be by

John Yenn, following a Chambersian scheme of twenty years earlier. It was in this room that the Queen held her drawing-rooms and ceremonies such as the reception of Richard Rush as American Ambassador in February 1818, and the marriage on 7th April that year of Princess Elizabeth to the Prince of Hesse-Homburg.

Apart from the Saloon there were two Drawing Rooms, both with painted ceilings, one designed by Chambers and the other by Adam, and in Pyne's day they contained splendid pictures, but perhaps the most fascinating room was the Queen's Breakfast Room (i). The Duke of Buckingham had had a Japan Room in the centre of the west front on the axis of the saloon, but this became the Crimson Drawing Room and the Queen decided to re-use the lacquer in the room to the south, the refitting being done by Vile in 1763. Between the windows Pyne shows pedimented mirrors made about 1740 which were also restored by Vile, and below them gilt gesso tables in the style of James Moore made about 1725, while the organ topped by a bust of Handel was that supplied by Bradburn in 1767.

However it is clear from the print that the room was done up in the early 19th century, and it is interesting to be able to compare its state with the very different impression it created in 1802. 'Here are the comforts of a family room, with the grandeur and some of the ornaments of a palace,' wrote a visitor that year. 'Three large paintings occupy three of the compartments, and several others leave not much place for the curious Japan lining, from which the room takes its name . . .' The curtains were painted in shades of brown and maroon, in imitation of cut velvet, by Princess Elizabeth, the tables and chairs were very plain and old fashioned, and 'the cold and hard-rubbed floor is without a carpet, a luxury of which his Majesty deprives himself in almost every apartment, for the opinion that carpets and other means of great warmth are injurious to health.' In other rooms the damask was much faded.

24

Pyne's impression is quite different: the big Van Dyck portraits have gone, and the room relies for its effect on the bold contrast of the black lacquer and the red continued drapery with its black gimp trimming, an idea probably derived from military fashions. The carpet with its diamond and urn motif is likely to have been of Brussels weave. Again, as in the library at Frogmore, the case covers on the chairs match the curtains and almost certainly the good upholstery they protect.

Although less and less time was spent at the Queen's House in the early 19th century, it was clearly kept up. Kensington Palace on the other hand was constantly raided for its contents, and Pyne's plate of the King's Gallery (*j*) came out after it had lost many of its pictures and not long before it was divided up for Princess Victoria. Originally constructed for William III and hung with green flowered velvet, it was altered in the 1720s by William Kent, who installed the chimneypiece and over-mantel and painted the ceiling with the story of Ulysses. The style of the curtain valances with their double scroll heads suggests that they date from the same time and so presumably the crimson did too. Pyne does not specify the material, but the pattern is so pronounced that it looks as if it were a cut velvet (probably wool velvet) rather than a damask. Between the window he shows great sconces and about the room are torchères that are similar to some still in the Royal Collection. The end of the gallery is dominated by Ricci's *Adoration*.

The final volume is devoted to St James's Palace and Carlton House. Fortunately Inigo Jones's chapel had survived the fire of 1809, but none of the other interiors, apart from the Queen's Library, was of particular interest from the point of view of architecture or decoration. However it was typical of Pyne's approach that he was not just concerned with what was grand and imposing, but liked to show lesser rooms like the Guard Chamber (*k*) and the Kitchen (*l*) as evidence of the character of the place.

The Drawing Room at St James's (detail) : *by Rowlandson and A. C. Pugin for Ackermann's 'Microcosm of London'*

St James's makes an understated prelude to Carlton House, to which Pyne devoted twenty plates. The interiors were the most spectacular in London, and in the view of Count Munster even the palace at St Petersburg was not equal to them in elegance or richness. As a series of plates they are the most important in the whole project, because they are such a marvellous record of increasingly extravagant decoration, but as Pyne gives no plan it is difficult to follow the lay-out of the house and indeed its architectural history. The Prince Regent began remodelling his grandmother's house with Holland, Chambers and Yenn as his architects, but Holland was out of favour after 1792 and finally left the scene in 1802. He was succeeded by Thomas Hopper, with Walsh Porter evidently supervising much of the decoration, but with some contributions from various members of the Wyatt family between 1804 and 1813. Finally that year Nash took over. Hopper's principal contribution was the gothic conservatory of 1807 and Nash's the gothic dining room of 1814, and the plates reproduced here appear to show Holland's interiors as overlaid by Walsh Porter or by upholsterers working after his death.

The Hall (*m*) was apparently the least altered of Holland's rooms, and Pyne shows its cross axis, the principal one being across from the outer hall to the Octagon, off which lay the staircase, and the First Ante-Chamber on the garden front. The general concept of the room recalls the staircase hall at Berrington in Herefordshire, also designed by Holland, and the disposition of columns appears on Holland's plan, but it is surely no accident that the screens of columns with urns were an idea taken up by the Wyatts at Tatton in Cheshire and that M. C. Wyatt was actually paid for painting eighteen bronzes in the Hall and Octagon in 1804. This suggests that the room as recorded by Pyne is not pure Holland, if only in the colour scheme. Holland with his French decorators had revived many techniques of painting that had been out of fashion for seventy years, and the Hall provided plenty of scope for different sorts of marbling, siena, porphyry, *verd antique* and bronze painting as well. The walls were granite green, the dado *verd antique*, the skirting porphyry; the siena marble columns carried a marbled entablature, with bases, capitals and additional ornaments bronzed. The frieze of the entablature was in simulated porphyry and bronze.

The history of the other main rooms is even more involved. The Crimson Drawing Room as shown by Pyne (*n*) is dominated by its early 19th-century hangings and upholstery, but in

27

fact it was evidently built, if not actually decorated, by 1787. As first completed it was used as the eating room, a function it fulfilled until 1804, when James Wyatt was involved in considerable but still undetermined alterations. Certainly the form of the room does not appear to have been changed, although it is known that the two chimneypieces were supplied by Benjamin Vulliamy in 1808, and it seems more than likely that he did not alter Holland's ceiling. On the other hand the emblems of tillage, harvest, vintage and field sports may tie up with designs made by Edward Wyatt. Be that as it may, certainly this was a case of the upholsterer winning out, for the walls, which were hung with British crimson satin damask, were virtually hidden by the festoons and valances of the same material hung from gilded Apollo heads attached to the cornice. The under-curtains for the windows were of white taffeta, a material which is unlikely to have lasted from 1804, and as the Prince of Wales was not the kind of man to simply replace what he had already, the date of the hangings is problematical. Beneath the drapery and the blaze of chandeliers, the pictures appear lost, but they included Rembrandt's *The Jewish Bride* and Rubens's *Landscape with St George*, a picture originally painted for Charles I and bought back by the Prince in 1814.

The Circular Room (*p*) which lay between the Crimson Drawing Room and the Throne Room was built a little later than its neighbours and was first intended as a music room, but was evidently used as a dining room in 1811 and is so identified on a plan of 1825. Despite the change of use, again it seems the bones of the decoration date back to the Holland period, and in the main it was the upholstery that was changed. Columns of *porfido rosso* scagliola by Bartoli are mentioned in 1789, and these would appear to be the same scagliola columns that are mentioned in 1811 and are shown in Pyne's view. The painting of the ceiling as sky, the arabesque painting round the mirrors and in the shutters, and the treatment of the doors and over-doors have been all attributed to Delabrière, one of the French

The Great Staircase, Kensington Palace (detail): *drawn by C. Wild*

decorators working with Holland: although to our ears the picking out in silver and the painting of ornaments to simulate bronze against a silver ground may sound bizarre, the use of bronze was not a rare feature of decoration at the turn of the century, whereas silver was used only occasionally for decorative work; it was rarely chosen in preference to gilding, being so short-lasting. And when it was used it naturally commanded the added appeal of extravagance. The draping of all the recesses with light blue silk to look like Roman tents with under-curtains of white taffeta was a piece of extravagance that could not have survived the use of the room for eating, and so presumably was done no more than five or six years before Pyne published his print, which was in 1817.

The extravagant revamping of Carlton House has been usually attributed to Walsh Porter, but as he died in 1809 and much of what Pyne shows must date from after that, it is not at all clear who directed the upholsterers. Nor do we know who designed the Blue Velvet Room (q), which was the Prince's private audience chamber. The conception of the ceiling painted as sky with panels symbolic of British naval and military triumphs and the Roman trophies on the doors could date back to the Holland period, but the emphasis on victory must surely date from after 1815. In the 1790s the Prince had been criticised for pursuing his admiration for French works of art, and it seems unlikely that he would have chosen to have the fleur-de-lis incorporated in his carpet and curtains before Waterloo. The walls were hung with dark blue velvet and the curtains had a broken drapery of blue satin embellished with fleur-de-lis of gold coloured satin lined with white taffeta. There was a great deal of gilding, but the woodwork instead of being white was painted 'light peach-blossom'. Against this rich, even over-rich background, it is hard to imagine how the pictures looked, but there were three great canvases, a Cuyp sea-picture, a Jan Both classical landscape and, most prominent of all, Rembrandt's *Portrait of a Ship-Builder and his Wife*, all three of which the Prince acquired in 1811.

No doubt it was a combination of flattery and commercial-
ism that led Pyne to devote so many plates to Carlton House,
but we should be grateful that he did what he did, and perhaps
one day his record will enable us to disentangle more
completely the development of the Prince's taste and changes
of mind.

Afterword

Pyne's plates have so much to tell, it seems odd that such records of interiors appear to be so rare. Certainly they were never particularly common in England and, as far as I can discover, the majority seem to have been done between 1800 and 1850 or 60. Few come up to the exacting standards set by Pyne, but it was a genre suited to the talents of the amateur who had profited to a greater or lesser extent from the instructions of a drawing master and was confined to the house by inclement weather. Most drawings come into this category, and indeed because of their lack of sophistication contain more information than Turner's brilliant watercolours of Petworth. Doubtless Pyne inspired many ladies to do their drawing rooms, and certainly Queen Victoria, who had an exacting sense of detail, saw the value of the plates as a record of the royal residences as they had been about the time of her birth and herself commissioned watercolours of interiors at Buckingham Palace and Balmoral as her own private record. A few have been reproduced and they take the story of those places on another generation, linking the time of her grandparents, George III and Queen Charlotte, and her uncle, George IV, with the age of photography; the age that was to kill the genre – and the drawing master.

(a) Queen Mary's State Bedchamber, Hampton Court   *Cattermole*

(c) The King's Audience Chamber, Windsor Castle

C. *Wild*

(e) The Queen's Library, Frogmore

C. Wild

PLATE 5

Stephanoff

(g) The Throne Room, Hampton Court

Stephanoff

(i) The Queen's Breakfast Room, Buckingham House

(k) The Guard Chamber, St James's

C. Wild

(m) The Hall of Entrance, Carlton House

C. Wild

(p) The Circular Room, Carlton House

C. *Wild*